Poems to Carry With You
On Life's Journey

Inspiration and Encouragement
For Every New Beginning

Poems to Carry With You
On Life's Journey

Inspiration and Encouragement
For Every New Beginning

by Bruce B. Wilmer

Published by:

Winding Brook Press

P. O. Box 7, Burnsville, NC 28714

This book is a compilation of new poems
and poems previously copyrighted by the author
in his books of poetry and
Light Lines® Originals poetry products

Cover photo and design by Bruce B. Wilmer

Photo of author by Sydney B. Wilmer,
as well as careful editing and
many helpful suggestions
as to content and organization

http://www.brucebwilmer.com

Printed in the United States of America

ISBN: 978-1-57158-002-3

*Dedicated to
the dreamers and believers,
the changers and challengers,
and all who are working to improve
themselves and the world*

INTRODUCTION

This collection, *Poems To Carry With You On Life's Journey,* grew out of my own journey through life and my attempts to find and shape my future. It is best characterized by the second poem in the book, "Follow Your Dreams," which I wrote for myself in 1976 at a time when my passion for writing poetry of all types was reaching critical mass and I didn't know how to proceed. Rebounding from jobs in a weak economy, my wife, Sydney, and I formed a poetry publishing business, Wilmer Graphics, in Huntington, New York in 1976, with virtually no capital and the added responsibility of a new baby.

For the first twelve years of the business, we also worked as live-in caretakers, maintaining the grounds of an estate while occupying its drafty 150-year-old carriage house apartment to defray living costs. That responsibility left us very busy on weekends and on countless workday evenings. With two young children to care for by 1981, leisure time was rare.

We started with two antiquated letter presses bought at auction and eventually graduated to modern in-house offset printing equipment with a full staff in production, design and sales. As a result of 36 years of considerable effort and determination, we have successfully marketed our poetry products in thousands of U.S. stores and 45 countries. During that time, I have authored hundreds of poems of love, friendship, family, inspiration, encouragement and communication, which have become the basis for our extensive group of Light Lines® Originals poetry products and books.

The road to these "dreams" was not easy or direct. I had to abandon a career path in law after being drafted into the Army in my first year of law school during the escalating Vietnam War (1968). The Army jump-started the writing avocation that was to become my career by compelling me in basic training and later military schooling to find a way to stay awake during large sleep-inducing lectures being patrolled by drill sergeants and lieutenants. I wrote humorous limericks about mind-numbing Army flow charts, acronyms, and many other subjects for diversion. After my advanced training at the US Army Intelligence School at Fort Holabird, Maryland, a choice secured by an extra year of enlistment, I had an unexpectedly long and interesting two-and-a-half year tour, joined by my wife, at the American Embassy in Bonn, Germany. This assignment gave me further time to cultivate my writing hobby in unusually fortunate circumstances, since I had been expecting my three year obligation to include a combat assignment in Vietnam after my initial 12 months in Germany.

Though my stay in the military deserves much credit for this accidental launch of my creative pursuits, my parents were the real spurs for all things creative. They were talented artists who lived and breathed creativity in everything they did. I lacked their gifts in painting and art and didn't go far enough in music, but followed the lure of their fascination for creative writing and poetry. My father was a gifted wordsmith who spent most of his working life as an advertising executive and commercial artist. It was not uncommon for our family to sit at the dinner table tossing around all kinds of ideas for names of products and schemes. We reveled in wordplay. My mother wrote poetry about everything that happened in her life and was the inspiration for my eventual fascination with poetry. Five years after my mother died, I challenged my father to celebrate his 90th birthday by collecting his previous writings into his own book of poetry. He surprised me by following through and completing the project with great skill and sincerity, proving you're never too old to follow your dreams.

There were other factors that gave me license to pursue an independent career path. I was influenced by the tenacity of two trailblazing uncles who left their home in Brooklyn, NY and moved to the west coast to pursue innovative careers, starting in the 1920's. One, Linwood G. Dunn, was an Academy Award winning pioneer of early cinema who has been called the "father of special effects." He animated the first King Kong, parted the Red Sea, launched the Starship Enterprise at warp speed in the original TV series, and generally mystified people with his thousand movie credits and complex special effects. It was hard for me to attend a movie without trying to guess how it was made. My other uncle, Lloyd W. Dunn, translated his family's passion for playing musical instruments into a career as a recording industry executive and pioneer who was one of the founders of the Grammy Awards and influential in hiring the Beatles. Their uncle, my great uncle, Spencer G. Bennet, was a hall of fame stuntman (who twice jumped death-defyingly from the NJ Palisades into the Hudson River), movie actor, and director of 122 films, including old westerns and the first Superman and Batman movies. He started his career in Thomas Edison's movie studios in 1912. These self-taught innovators, along with my highly creative parents, left me with the feeling that no career path was out of the ordinary or beyond imagining.

Teachers and professors also played important roles by helping me to believe in myself while challenging any traces of complacency. My strict eighth grade teacher, who drilled us with grammar rules and creative writing assignments, told my parents that I should become a writer some day. Her goodhearted remark and belief in me was something I have always wanted to justify. Four years later, my sweet, soft-spoken English 12 Honors teacher ripped my creative writing apart with worthwhile criticism and killed any illusions I might have had about creative writing being a cakewalk. Nevertheless, she urged me to submit my earliest serious poem to the school literary journal, and this became my first published poem.

At the University of Rochester, it was Professor Norman O. Brown's course in "Archetypes" that made all the difference and gave me an approach to my later writing. The important words of encouragement and challenge I received from this innovative scholar—who has since been labeled "the philosopher of the sixties"—raised my creative bar to the very top rung. His poetic archetypes remain my elusive goal as I try to portray the specifics of human experience in more general terms through my inspirational and purposeful poetry. Interestingly, he concludes his famous 1966 book, *Love's Body*, with the observation: "There is only poetry." Obviously I believed him.

It was after publication of my first book of light verse, *High On A Limerick*, in 1974, while working in the White Mountains of New Hampshire following my return from military service, that an open-minded managing editor of a national newspaper gave my poetry column a byline on the back page of his newspaper. While my subsequent attempt to syndicate the column nationally failed, I was excited at my first real chance to reach a large audience of readers with my poetic efforts. This start 38 years ago was followed by many other new beginnings. I discovered early on that I had to be patient in pursuing my goals and prepared to take it one step at a time.

Each life's journey, including mine, is dynamic, full of dreams, choices, successes and regrets. Life turns on small things as well as large. There are high points and low points, milestones and moments of challenge, times to remember and times to forget...or, better, to learn from. Chance and choice are partners. Luck and labor intersect. It is my hope that among these 77 poems will be one or more that will comfort you on your journey and encourage you to make a difference to yourself or another. My goal is to provide "a gentle nudge in a positive direction" and in some small way to help you to *follow your dreams*.

—Bruce B. Wilmer
Western NC (2012)

CONTENTS

You may seek all the answers:
 Be content to find a few.
Don't grow impatient with the world—
 Tomorrow's world is you.

from Tomorrow's World Is You (page 9)

Poems to Carry With You

On Life's Journey

Follow Your Dreams

BELIEVE IN YOURSELF

Believe in yourself
　　To the depth of your being.
Nourish the talents
　　Your spirit is freeing.

Know in your heart
　　When the going gets slow
That your faith in yourself
　　Will continue to grow.

Don't forfeit ambition
　　When others may doubt.
It's your life to live—
　　You must live it throughout.

Learn from your errors—
　　Don't dwell in the past.
Never withdraw
　　From a world that is vast.

Believe in yourself;
　　Find the best that is you.
Let your spirit prevail;
　　Steer a course that is true.

FOLLOW YOUR DREAMS

If while pursuing distant dreams
    Your bright hopes turn to gray,
Don't wait for reassuring words
    Or hands to lead the way.

For seldom will you find a soul
    With dreams the same as yours.
Not often will another help you
    Pass through untried doors.

If inner forces urge you
    To take a course unknown,
Be ready to go all the way,
    Yes, all the way alone.

That's not to say you shouldn't
    Draw lessons from the best;
Just don't depend on lauding words
    To spur you on your quest.

Find confidence within your heart
    And let it be your guide.
Strive ever harder toward your dreams
    And they won't be denied.

NEW BEGINNINGS

Each chapter that is ending
   Leads us to a new beginning.
The past that we are leaving
   Means a future we are winning.

Each change that fills the present
   Sets the stage for our tomorrow,
And how we meet each challenge
   Helps determine joy or sorrow.

In every new beginning
   Spirit plays a vital part.
We must approach tomorrow
   With a strong and steady heart.

So as we turn the corner
   Let's all apprehension shed
And fill our hearts with confidence
   As we proceed ahead.

ALWAYS HAVE A GOAL

The goal is there for all to see—
    The measure of the game.
We're on the field somewhere between
    The failure and the fame.

We try our best to move the ball
    Through patterns, plays and passes.
The goal seems near or far away
    Through our subjective glasses.

The game may be an endless quest,
    More losses than advances.
The goal may always loom right there
    Eluding all our chances.

We may not ever cross the line;
    We may not win the praise;
We may not see our struggles end,
    Nor see triumphant days.

But better to have sought the challenge,
    Better to have tried,
Better to have found the courage
    Dwelling deep inside.

The people from the sidelines
    May judge harshly each mistake;
But should you snare the victory,
    They'll share the winner's cake.

So better risk a contest lost
    Than brood of skills forsaken.
The victories will only come
    When challenges are taken.

The energy it takes to quell
    Ambitions from within
Is often more than it would take
    To grab the ball and win.

So if we summon from our hearts
    Those strengths we seldom use,
We'll be a victor in the toughest
    Contest, win or lose!

THE ART OF LIVING

Our life is but a canvas—
　　We're artists of a kind.
As we apply the brush strokes,
　　Life's meaning is defined.

We can play the role of master—
　　Fill in details of our own—
Or let the paint flow randomly,
　　Let chance decide the tone.

We can choose each color wisely—
　　Just as friends are picked with care—
Or let all those around us
　　Merely place the colors there.

We can look behind us proudly
　　At the stages of our art
Or see a life unfolding
　　In which we play little part.

Though our life is but a canvas,
　　There is much that we can do
To make it our best work of art—
　　And our creation, too.

TOMORROW'S WORLD IS YOU

Your world is changing faster now.
    Your choices are unfolding.
The future lies within your grasp,
    A vital force worth molding.

Your role is not a simple one;
    Your course has not been set.
You must avoid the obstacles,
    Steer clear of every threat.

The pressures come from all around—
    Examples good and bad.
Be richer through the friends you choose,
    The peers who strengthen, add.

Accept responsibility.
    Deserve your parents' trust.
Let go of your dependence—
    Temper freedom's forward thrust.

Don't ever lose control
    And let the others steer your course.
Your life's a gift for you to shape
    With independent force.

Reach high; pursue your talents;
 Make the most of your potential.
Remember, as your goals take form,
 Your dreams become essential.

You may seek all the answers:
 Be content to find a few.
Don't grow impatient with the world—
 Tomorrow's world is you.

THE FUTURE IS YOURS

I look to you with hope and pride;
    I see your future brightly.
Your deep concerns and aspirations
    I will not take lightly.

The future is a mystery
    That everyone explores.
I'll share your possibilities,
    Embrace your distant shores.

I'll answer you when questions stir,
    Encourage you, implore you.
But life's a challenge shaped by dreams,
    A gift I can't live for you.

So live it well; respect it fully;
    Play your spirit out.
Seek and then discover
    All the best that life's about.

Remember that you're not alone—
    My love is always there.
The challenge that defines your life
    My heart will gladly share.

You're on a voyage into time,
A trip to somewhere new.
You may not always see me there,
But I'll be there with you.

FIND YOUR DESTINY

Find your future;
    Set it free.
Strive to shape
    Your destiny.

Find a path
    Among the choices.
Live to learn;
    Enlist wise voices.

Seek a purpose;
    Frame a goal;
Embrace a standard;
    Shape a role.

Discover heart;
    Uncover strength.
Involve yourself
    To any length.

Look for sun;
    Accept the rain.
Cherish joy;
    Resolve the pain.

Immerse in spirit;
    Seize the hour;
Keep your faith
    And let it flower.

Listen to the winds
    Now blowing.
Destiny is
    Where you're going.

DREAM A NEW DAY

Life is a trail
   With a wonderful view,
But the path may not always
   Be easy for you.

You'll gaze at the peak
   From the place where you stand
And try to approach it
   In ways you have planned.

Time will decide
   If your route is the best,
If you can negotiate
   Every steep test.

Yet, life is an endless
   Assortment of views—
New paths, new approaches,
   New summits to choose.

And if a past vision
   You have to revise,
Another will greet you
   Just over the rise:

Another objective,
Another grand view,
Another firm purpose
To motivate you.

So take on the challenge;
Reach out for a way;
Expand the adventure;
And dream a new day.

ANYTHING IS POSSIBLE

Never doubt your own potential.
  Never lose your motivation.
Never give up your objectives.
  Never hide in hesitation.

You can choose your own direction.
  You can plot a better course.
You can find a new beginning.
  You can tap an inner force.

Anything can be accomplished.
  Any challenge can be met,
Any negative surmounted,
  Any obstacle upset.

Life is full of reasons not to
  Do the things you dream of doing.
Find a goal that you can seize
  With energy and start pursuing.

Draw upon your inspiration.
  Fill your faith up to the top.
Move ahead with constant effort.
  Stay on course and never stop.

MAKE IT HAPPEN

When you want to move ahead
    And trade new patterns for the old
And take with you the lessons learned
    And let a whole new life unfold,
                Make it happen!

When the past has served its purpose,
    Helped define your hopes and dreams,
You can shape a new tomorrow
    Brighter than today now seems.
                Make it happen!

You must bring a new perspective,
    Build a healthy attitude.
You must ride your confidence
    Beyond a pessimistic mood.
                Make it happen!

Take the present in your hands
    And shape it like tomorrow's clay.
The future will in time become
    The better life you live today.
                Make it happen!

THE ANSWER LIES WITHIN

Certain questions
    Are the tough ones,
Such as how does
    Change begin.

Often no one
    Can assist you,
Since the answer
    Lies within.

You must make
    The tough decisions.
You must delve
    Into your mind.

You must see
    Where you are wisest.
You must see
    Where you are blind.

You must make
    A plan to follow.
You must take
    A step to start.

You must summon
    All your talents.
You must mobilize
    Your heart.

GO FOR IT!

Shake off your doubts and then go for it.
Check out your options and act.
Find an approach to the future,
And turn today's dreams into fact.

Take a first step to tomorrow.
Start on the course of your choice.
Look at what life has to offer.
Listen to your inner voice.

Don't live a life of regretting,
Stifled by negative force.
Think of what you can accomplish.
Steer an affirmative course.

Build on activities positive.
Work with abundance of heart.
By making the best of the present,
Change is the process you start.

Even though problems may surface,
Problems don't have to prevail
As long as you're one who is trying
And never just waiting to fail.

WHAT IS SUCCESS?

Success is measured day by day—
    It's life that's lived, not squandered.
It's problems solved, meanings found,
    And not just futures pondered.

It's sorting out our hopes and dreams
    From visions all too fleeting.
It's choosing goals within our means,
    Not projects self-defeating.

It's loving self and others, too;
    It's finding peace in duty.
It's sensing harmony in life
    And seeing nature's beauty.

It's living life for all it's worth,
    Not fearful of tomorrow.
It's accepting all that's gone before,
    Not dwelling in past sorrow.

Success is measured not by wealth;
    It's there for rich or poor.
For all who give each day their best
    It leaves an open door.

IF YOU NEVER TRY

If you never try,
    You'll never have to face defeat.
If you never run a race,
    You'll never lose a heat.

If you never stretch your talents,
    You won't risk a tear.
If you never take a chance,
    The odds you'll never fear.

But if you have a lifelong wish
    And you don't venture out,
You will never overcome
    Uncertainty and doubt.

And if you have a goal to reach
    And time is passing by,
You will never know fulfillment
    If you never try.

MAKE YOUR OWN LUCK

Though luck is a thing you can wait for,
    Just hoping the future will change,
Good fortune is really a shy one—
    Each meeting you have to arrange.

Tomorrow can come and then vanish,
    Its vast possibilities gone,
If you avoid each day's potential
    And let it slip by with a yawn.

There's always some risk when you're trying,
    Some failures for those who set goals;
But no one was meant to be perfect,
    And learning is one of life's roles.

Luck is a force you must work for—
    Tomorrow's a gift you must find.
Today is the first step you're taking
    Toward a future that's better defined.

Good fortune will never embrace you
    If you sit there sulking or smug.
But seek it; pursue it; and reach out to find it;
    And give every setback a shrug.

YOU'RE A WORK IN PROGRESS

You've got a future full of dreams,
    A world of things undone.
You're still a work in progress
    With a theme that's just begun.

Each day can bring rewards
    If you embrace each day with wonder.
Every storm conceals
    A hidden sun beyond its thunder.

Challenges can be much more
    Than contests meant for winning.
Every fresh experience
    Can yield a new beginning.

Life has possibilities,
    Rich moments to explore.
Observing life too passively
    Can be a downright bore.

You can find the vast potential
    Hidden in each day.
You can give it meaning
    In your own distinctive way.

You can sense life's promise,
    Even when you're feeling low.
You're still a work unfinished
    With a long, long way to go.

SUCCESS

You can measure success
    In terms of the past,
Noting chances you've seized
    Or have wasted.

By just looking back,
    You can linger in memories
Of fortunes you've missed
    Or have tasted.

You can measure success
    In terms of the future—
Elusive, forever
    Tomorrow.

You can always be sure
    That it lurks just ahead
And in dreams find the cure
    For all sorrow.

You can measure success
    In terms of the present
And live your life fully
    Each day;

For success doesn't dwell
    In your memories or dreams
But in steps that you take
    On the way.

Be Yourself

BE YOURSELF

The world would like to change you;
    There are pressures all around.
You must decide just who you are,
    Then firmly hold your ground.

You have an image of yourself,
    An ideal sense of you;
And to this vision you must always
    Struggle to be true.

You know what you are good at,
    And you know where talents lie;
But if you're ruled by others,
    Your uniqueness could pass by.

Remember there is much to learn;
    But all new things aren't good.
Wisdom lies in what you've learned
    And what you have withstood.

So, be yourself and don't allow
    The world to take control.
Preserving your identity
    Is life's most precious goal.

LISTEN TO YOUR HEART

Some won't understand you
Or accept the path you're on.
Some will try to change you,
Leave your sense of purpose gone.

Some will feel you have to live
Up to their expectations.
Some will live your life for you,
Ignore your aspirations.

They may drain your energy
And leave your spirit weak,
But you must keep remembering
The ways you are unique.

You must let your sense of self
Defeat their sense of you.
You must try to be secure
With your own point of view.

If your future path is one
That you would like to chart,
Search for your identity
And listen to your heart.

JUST ONCE

I gazed upon my life
    And sensed its rush before my time.
I saw my youth dissolving
    Long before I met my prime.

I felt the moment slipping by,
    My stay on earth depleting.
I saw the present hurrying,
    My mortal cares repeating.

I feared that I would squander time
    And miss my only chance.
I didn't want to waste
    The opportunity life grants.

We occupy this planet
    For a brief allotted hour,
And there exists within each heart
    A reservoir of power.

My hope is to define it well,
    Try not to let it slide.
My challenge is to pull some meaning
    From this force inside.

Sitting near the edge of time,
My mind forever hunts
To justify the simple truth—
We pass this way just once.

IDENTITY PRAYER

Let me live and let me love
    And let me flourish free.
Let me be a total person—
    Let me know I'm me.

Let me grow and let me change
    To reach my true potential.
Let me choose important things,
    Reject the nonessential.

Let me listen, let me see
    The truths that others bring.
Let me savor human warmth—
    Let me laugh and sing.

Let me be secure enough
    To state my wants and needs.
Let me have enough to give
    Through words as well as deeds.

Let me find out who I am,
    Explore my definition.
Let me be in my own way
    A vital first edition!

MAKE TODAY COUNT

Today's important; make it count.
    Find courage for each test.
Be alert; and be involved;
    And always be your best.

You fill a slot, assume a job,
    Take on a task or role;
But don't just give a portion of yourself—
    Present the whole.

By holding back or being
    Somewhere else when you are there,
Your presence is a compromise
    Of all you have to share.

If you can fill a moment
    With desire and with heart
And you can occupy your space
    By really taking part,

The present will return to you
    The dividends you're due.
Today will count much more
    If you'll just give the best of you.

TRUST

Throughout our relationships,
  One concept is a must:
Things can go much farther
  If they're firmly based on trust.

Trust is something subtle—
  It's an underlying theme.
It fortifies a world where things
  Aren't always what they seem.

Trust is built up over time—
  Its precious faith is learned.
Honesty applied to life
  Is how this gift is earned.

Trust assigns a higher weight
  To every promise spoken.
It can build so much while there,
  So little when it's broken.

Trust is that sure link between
  The truth and what is heard.
Trust is simply how you back
  The value of your word.

FOLLOW YOUR HEART

In the depth of your being,
 In a place in the heart,
There are times when your reason
 And feeling must part.

Your logic directs you
 To follow one course,
But your innermost feeling
 Applies a firm force.

When instinct and reason
 Diverge and divide,
You must sometimes respond
 To that feeling inside.

For your heart in the end
 Is a much sterner judge
Of a reason that clings
 To a mind that won't budge.

And since life unfolds
 As the subtlest art,
There are times when you clearly
 Must follow your heart.

YOU CAN MAKE A DIFFERENCE

You can make a difference
  In your corner of the earth.
You can reach for higher goals,
  Encourage human worth.

You can help the others
  To accomplish all they should.
You can find a way
  To reinforce the cause of good.

You can try to understand
  The problems of the few.
You can be a voice of kindness
  Gently passing through.

You can search for purpose
  In the many tasks of man.
If you choose to make a difference,
  You're the one who can.

BE A SOURCE OF LIGHT

In the darkness,
    In the shadows,
In the cold
    Of night,

You can be a source
    Of spirit—
You can be a
    Light.

You can radiate
    Your caring.
You can share
    Your flame.

You can add
    Your energy,
Abandoned hopes
    Reclaim.

You can be a source
    Of strength,
A bridge to
    Higher goals.

You can be a beacon
    Bright,
A guide to
    Weary souls.

TAKE PRIDE IN YOUR WORK

No one can force you
    To carry inside
A standard of caring,
    A measure of pride.

You must decide
    Whether you will protect
A quality image
    That breeds self-respect.

You know the truth
    That your conscience proclaims
When you do a job
    That ennobles or shames.

You know when compromise
    Makes you fall shy.
You also know when
    Your standards are high.

You can't fool yourself—
    You're the one who knows first
When your job is the best
    Or your job is the worst.

Others may settle
    For just getting by—
You can be one of
    Those rare ones who try.

Some take up space,
    Filling jobs that they shirk.
You can be one
    Who takes pride in his work.

BE KIND TO YOURSELF

You're constantly exposed
    To daily obstacles and stress.
You're steadily upgrading
    Your own measures of success.

You try to heed the message
    Of ambition and of hope;
But you may tackle mountains
    Where you can't foresee the slope.

You tend to be too hard
    Upon yourself when you fall short.
By stretching out too far,
    You make success a losing sport.

You must be kinder to yourself,
    See life in different ways.
Perfection is a tempting goal
    That teases and dismays.

Just build upon what you can do—
    Select a path that's real.
Understand your limitations—
    Summon what you feel.

Redefine your expectations—
Let your future flow.
A little patience with yourself
Will keep your dreams aglow.

THE CREATIVE PERSON

You're the one who has the spark,
  Who keeps the ideas flowing,
Whose bright imagination
  Helps to keep the pace from slowing.

You're the one who has the gift,
  Who searches without ceasing,
Whose inspiration always
  Through hard effort is increasing.

You're the one who has the drive,
  Who struggles to uncover
All that acquiescent minds
  Aren't likely to discover.

You're the one who sorts the choices,
  Seeks the combinations,
And drawing from your boundless spirit
  Yields the innovations.

You're the one pursuing goals
  Your talents can immerse in.
In your unique, distinctive way,
  You're the creative person.

SO EASY TO LOSE

A soft inner flame
    Licks the air,
Asking the moment
    For a lull
In which to reach up
    And exist.

A terse, taunting
    Wind
Whips the shy energy
    At its roots.

Breeze after breeze
    Dims its glow,
As purpose genuflects
    To nipping challenge.

No lull lets
    Spirit soar:
All hell would rather
    Consume it.

In this hostile air,
    All bright ideas
Must somehow fare…
    Or fall quiet.

In assaulting
    Gust and gale,
A force will find
    Its anchors on the fly

And purpose will survive
    Its lonely fight
And life will let
    A dream ignite

Or, in the press
    Of vagaries that flow,
Will let it die,
    An eager light
That loved so much
    To grow.

GIVE EVERY MOMENT YOUR BEST

When you're starting to work
    On a tedious task
And your energy's
    Fading away,
Give a bit more
    Than the job may entail—
Put some energy
    Into your day.

Don't be content
    With the minimum effort,
The least that
    A person can do.
Tackle the moment
    With more than enough—
You'll find there's
    A lot more in you.

There's only one life—
    It's your treasure to carry;
So live it and
    Breathe it with zest.
Don't ever squander
    The meagerest portion—
Give every moment
    Your best.

BE A LEADER

At times when the values
    Of others seem hollow,
Make sure that you're ready
    To lead and not follow.

It's not always easy
    To challenge the crowd
Or stick to your views
    When opponents are loud;

But sometimes a group
    Tends to lose its direction
And goes down a path
    Sorely needing correction.

Though opting for change
    Leaves you open to scorn,
Don't stand undecided,
    Divided or torn.

You're merely respecting
    Companions and friends
By searching for wisdom
    When common sense ends.

So if your group needs
    Better aims to pursue,
Your guidance can furnish
    The right thing to do.

When actions of others
    Aren't apt to succeed,
Don't give in and follow—
    Step forward and lead.

STEADY DOES IT

Genius may attract attention;
    Talent turns the eyes.
But hard work always proves to us
    That steady takes the prize.

Brilliance may find ways to dazzle;
    Quickness may astound.
But in the end results determine
    Where success is found.

High potential stirs our hopes;
    Credentials may impress.
But good performance overshadows
    What these gifts express.

When it comes to measuring
    How victories are won,
We disregard the promises
    And look to what's been done.

And when we try to track
    How true achievement is inspired,
A steady, honest effort
    Seems the talent most required.

I AM ME (WYSIWYG)

I am me—I'm what you see.
    I'm pure originality.
I'm some of this, a bit of that;
    I'm new and changing—not old hat.

No one ever has to gripe
    Because I fill a stereotype.
I'm strong inside and I am proud—
    I need not blend into the crowd.

What You See Is What You Get.
    I shape myself without regret.
My full description can't be known—
    You'll never find me cut in stone.

I'm different; I'm unique; I'm me.
    I'm what you might call label-free.
Yes, to myself I'm always true—
    That wondrous freedom life grants you!

Don't Give Up

DON'T GIVE UP

The path to higher goals in life
　　May not be smooth and clear.
At times you may experience
　　Frustration or a tear.

You may endure a setback,
　　Lose momentum, tumble down.
A former look of confidence
　　May turn into a frown.

With any goal that's worth achieving
　　Strength of heart will matter.
Nothing's ever handed out
　　Upon a silver platter.

Such a challenge draws upon
　　The very best of you,
Bringing into focus
　　The objectives you pursue.

And if you have to reconsider
　　How you will proceed,
You'll have stores of new self-knowledge
　　You can wisely heed.

And you can say that setbacks
    May have made the going slow;
But they have also given you
    Some valued time to grow.

I BELIEVE IN YOU

The challenges you now confront
    In all you're going through
Help me see the many ways
    That I believe in you.

It's hard for me to realize
    The things that you must face;
And though I try I can't completely
    Step into your place.

But something in my knowledge
    Of the depth and soul of you
Gives to every real concern
    An optimistic hue.

For when you must respond to life
    With pure determination,
Your answer to the challenge
    Is a source of inspiration.

And though each day's uncertainty
    The future oft obscures,
My hope for you is strong
    And my belief in you endures.

TAKE CHARGE OF YOUR LIFE

If you feel that life is getting
    Out of your control
And you are just existing
    With no trace of plan or goal,

Don't feel that you're alone
    In your uncertainty and strife;
Work hard to find a better course—
    Take charge of your own life.

Don't wallow in the currents
    Of a life without direction.
Don't tolerate a mental state
    Of crippling introspection.

Don't be a helpless passenger
    Of random circumstance.
Become the driver in your life,
    The governor of chance.

Don't ever act abruptly
    Or proceed without a plan;
If you but have a goal to reach,
    There is a chance you can.

The range of future choices
    Always will appear quite large;
But you will have a greater say
    If you will just take charge.

YOU FACE A SPECIAL CHALLENGE

Many things require extra work
    And years of trying.
Every challenge offers hope
    Of changes gratifying.

What you've undertaken
    Takes a lot of drive and force.
You are on a difficult
    And stimulating course.

I admire your attempt
    To reach your chosen goal.
You'll require discipline
    As well as self-control.

Every day you keep on trying
    Makes you that much stronger.
Obstacles, a part of growth,
    May make the trip seem longer.

But be assured all effort brings
    A form of satisfaction.
You will learn to go beyond
    And master each distraction.

Nothing in this world can make
Your future seem so whole
As knowing you are reaching for
A most demanding goal.

TAKE IT ONE STEP AT A TIME

It's true that sometimes life is full
    Of trying circumstances,
And sometimes we must struggle
    For just minimal advances.

Despite events that slow us down
    And magnify our worries,
We must learn that progress is
    A word that seldom hurries.

To try to grasp the total picture
    Is a strong temptation.
Often we attempt too much
    And add to our frustration.

Laying out before us
    All the things that must be done
May be harder than to focus
    On a single one.

Don't approach so many tasks
    That all your hopes are gone.
A single step will lead you to
    Another later on.

THAT STRENGTH FROM WITHIN

When problems beset us
    Or trials begin,
Let's summon that power,
    That strength from within.

It's there when we need it;
    It flows from the heart.
It's the noblest energy
    Life can impart.

It says: Never weaken—
    Don't ever give in.
With invincible spirit
    Keep striving to win.

Though the odds may seem heavy
    And the effort seem great,
The courage we muster
    Will govern our fate.

So acknowledge the challenge—
    Then give it your best.
Let that strength from within
    Help you meet every test.

LIFE ISN'T ALWAYS EASY

Life has its trials and obstacles,
Its measure of setbacks and spills.
Life has its true disappointments,
Its mountains that start out as hills.

Sometimes we can't find the answers.
Often we end up depressed.
Frequently we have the feeling
That life is a terrible test.

Simple solutions elude us.
Difficult questions remain.
Thought is a lingering burden,
A well of emotional pain.

Nevertheless there's a dignity
That we eventually find,
Born of a growing awareness
Of victories won in the mind.

No battles can ever be greater
Than those that may never be won.
The fact that you've gallantly struggled
Is one fact that can't be undone.

The past is a bundle of memories
Infusing the present with tears.
But you are that person courageous
Who valiantly still perseveres.

IT'S HOW YOU COPE

Life has its measure of setbacks—
    Some are small, some are larger in size.
There are portions of every existence
    Which clearly we'd like to revise.

But stresses and problems are normal—
    Disappointments are part of the game.
If we let these moments control us,
    We must assume part of the blame.

It's how we react that's important;
    We mustn't distort what we feel.
Let's work with what life has to offer
    And never begrudge a bad deal.

Depression can never assist us
    In weathering woes on this earth.
We shouldn't let each disappointment
    Give rise to more grief than it's worth.

Instead we should try to discover,
    As life in intensity mounts,
A way to place things in proportion.
    You see, how we cope is what counts.

TRY TO GET OVER IT

Life can sometimes
    Taunt and tease you.
Things don't always
    Go your way.

Plans are made
    And hopes created—
Still your steps
    May go astray.

Don't anticipate
    Perfection.
Don't expect
    A path unmarred.

For life's troubling
    Spills and setbacks
You should always
    Be on guard.

Take your daily
    Dose of challenge.
Take your large
    And small frustration.

Move ahead;
    Get over it;
Go forward with
    Determination.

YES I CAN!

When I need to face tomorrow,
　　Figure out a better way,
Settle on some goals to guide me,
　　Struggle onward, then I'll say,
　　　　　　　　Yes I can!

When I must confront a challenge,
　　When I have to deal with doubt,
When I want to shape the future,
　　When I'm forced to work it out,
　　　　　　　　Yes I can!

When the pace is going slower,
　　When results are tough to find,
When I must work hard for changes,
　　Tapping powers of the mind,
　　　　　　　　Yes I can!

Life will not defeat my spirit—
　　Life won't let my courage wane.
I will always keep on trying,
　　Finding hope in this refrain—
　　　　　　　　Yes I can!

GIVE IT YOUR BEST

There are times when life is tough,
    When trials are the worst.
There are special challenges
    When fortunes seem reversed.

Life delivers problems
    That are harder to explain.
Certain situations
    Cause a larger share of pain.

But out of all the trials
    Flows a stronger side of you.
There are crucial goals
    You must continue to pursue.

You must confront the obstacles;
    You must defeat the doubts;
You must persist when giving up
    Is all the moment shouts.

And when you reach the final stages
    Of a lengthy test,
You'll be a victor of the heart,
    Because you did your best.

THE HUMAN SPIRIT

The human spirit lifts a life,
   The problems it repels.
The human spirit offers courage
   Through the storms and swells.

The human spirit will not yield
   To failure's crushing ways.
The human spirit has to look
   Beyond its yesterdays.

The human spirit learns to deal
   With ever-present changes.
Hope is what the human spirit
   Quietly arranges.

The human spirit meets its test
   When tragedy arrives.
Giving up is not a choice
   When human spirit thrives.

In the darkest hours
   When a hurt is in the heart,
One survives because
   The human spirit plays a part.

To all who doubt its major role
And question if it's there,
Search the mind of humankind—
Its force is everywhere.

IF YOU HAVE A PROBLEM

If you have a problem
   That bothers you inside
And time does little to assure you
   That it will subside,

Then draw upon your inner strength
   And formulate a plan;
And every time you think you can't,
   Remember that you can.

Listen to your deepest voice
   Where reason still remains,
And take control of your own life
   To minimize the strains.

Strip away the fantasies,
   The negatives, the doubts,
The anger, the hostility,
   And guilt's recurrent bouts.

Try to shift into a course
   That's positive in tone.
Communicate your feelings
   So that you are not alone.

A pattern of improvement
    Is the change that you'll be winning
If you'll just let a single step
    Become a new beginning.

WHEN YOU'RE FEELING DOWN

When you're feeling down,
    Attempt to understand your mind.
When you've lost your dreams,
    There is a purpose you must find.

When your burdens weaken you
    And bend your form to breaking,
Try to shape a new approach
    To ease your inner aching.

When despair defines your path,
    Assigns a steeper slope,
You must find a way
    To keep on rushing back to hope.

When depression seems to be
    An unrelenting force,
Search for feelings positive
    And try to learn their source.

When you sense that progress is
    A dream that's hard to move,
Boost your life with expectation—
    Struggle to improve.

Let a little optimism
    Challenge every frown.
Find a goal and make it happen,
    When you're feeling down.

JUST HANG ON

In all the times that seem so hard
    When tears cry out inside,
You must explore new ways to live,
    Reverse depression's tide.

When all of your solutions
    Stay away, remain unknown,
And you are isolated
    In your heart and feel alone,

Remember that the world
    Is full of others just like you;
And you can reach beyond the darkness,
    Change your point of view.

Everyone has moments
    When their problems seem too much.
Everyone has joys that seem
    Elusive, out of touch.

But when it all seems very bleak
    And hope has all but gone,
Remember, time will heal your heavy thoughts
    If you'll hang on.

THINGS WILL GET BETTER

When things aren't going well for you
    And times aren't what they should be,
Just focus on the positive
    And think about what could be.

Acknowledge what has happened—
    Don't lose sight of lessons past—
But don't allow the negative
    Distracting thoughts to last.

Take what you've learned and start from there;
    Draw strength from your frustration;
And let this added sense of purpose
    Be your new foundation.

It's hard to follow any plan
    Precisely to the letter.
Though life right now is difficult,
    Things will in time get better.

TURN IT AROUND

Whenever something jarring happens,
    Turns things upside down,
Never let this problem win;
    Don't settle for a frown—
            Turn it around.

When there's no good answer
    For misfortune's callous course
And life endures a setback
    Or confronts a hostile force,
            Turn it around.

Every cloud that passes over,
    Covering the sun,
Cannot last forever;
    Soon its shadow will be done—
            Turn it around.

Certain opportunities
    Are hidden in your grief.
They can be discovered
    In the strength of your belief—
            Turn it around.

The past is now behind you,
  And the future lies ahead.
There is cause for optimism
  If you cast off dread—
              Turn it around.

FIND YOUR SPIRIT

When your life
  Has lost direction,
When your purpose
  Has no force,

When your day is
  Lacking meaning,
You must find
  Your spirit's source.

You must craft
  A new beginning;
You must find
  A way to start;

You must stir again
  Your interest;
You must redirect
  Your heart.

Everyone has
  Precious spirit
Tucked away
  Deep down inside.

You'll discover
	In your search—
Your spirit can't
	Forever hide.

KEEP THE FAITH!

When the world seems bleak around you,
    When concerns and fears surround you,
When tomorrow's dreams are hurting—
    News and views are disconcerting—
                Keep the faith!

When morale just keeps on sinking,
    Confidence is ever shrinking,
Future prospects leave you leery,
    Just surviving makes you weary,
                Keep the faith!

When the daily forecasts worsen,
    Shocking each and every person,
Hope is getting hard to muster,
    Striving hard has lost its luster,
                Keep the faith!

Don't surrender your ambition—
    Shape a purpose; find a mission.
Don't give up the current battle.
    Put yourself back in the saddle.
                Keep the faith!

Now's the time for change and action—
    Tackle your dissatisfaction.
You will find the inspiration
    To improve your situation.
                 Keep the faith!

YOU HAVE THE POWER

You have the power to address
　　The problems in your life.
You have the strength to get beyond
　　The challenges and strife.

Deep inside you'll find the will,
　　The pure determination.
You will shape a new beginning,
　　Start your transformation.

Nothing is so difficult,
　　No obstacle so great,
That you can't intervene and take
　　Command of your own fate.

Set your goals and understand
　　Your strengths and limitations.
Move ahead and tap the power
　　Of great expectations.

BELIEVE IN TOMORROW

Every day
    You're moving forward.
All decisions past
    Are done.

All your choices
    Lie before you.
New directions
    Are begun.

All your errors
    Will not vanish.
All regrets won't be
    Erased.

Life is lived
    But once, and sadly
It can never be
    Retraced.

You can try to live
    It better.
You can learn from
    Your mistakes.

You can build
    A new tomorrow,
Even if the past
    Still aches.

FIND A MIRACLE

Start each day
    With newfound purpose—
Set objectives
    Higher.

Find a way
    To tap your spirit,
Amplify
    Your fire.

You can shape
    A new beginning
From the hopes
    You carry.

Turn them into
    Something rare,
Beyond the
    Ordinary.

Take the very
    Best of you,
Envision something
    Bold.

Change your life
And let a
Little miracle
Unfold.

The Promise Of Today

THE PROMISE OF TODAY

Today you're heading toward the future,
   Moving from the past.
Tomorrow's filled with raw potential,
   Purpose that can last.

Today's a new beginning,
   Drawing lessons from before.
Morning is a new horizon
   With so much in store.

Shape the day; release the past.
   Your present gift is now.
Don't despair that yesterday
   Will seldom tell you how.

Make each day a challenge
   To be tackled with your heart.
Make each day a choice in which
   You're really taking part.

Don't expect a miracle—
   All change is hard and slow.
Merely learn that progress is
   A better way to go.

By choosing to reverse
    A backward trend, the future molding,
You can thrill to something great,
    A miracle unfolding.

And if you need some evidence
    That says you've found the way,
Try noticing the living proof—
    The promise of today.

TOMORROW'S CHOICES

As you move to shape your life
    And hear tomorrow's voices,
You will see in all its varied forms
    A world of choices.

You are many-faceted,
    With interests, skills, and talents.
You must find direction,
    Scan your options, maintain balance.

Life advances step-by-step,
    A book for time to read.
You must make decisions
    Based upon your current need.

You will answer challenges,
    Explore new paths each day.
You will make discoveries,
    Adjust in your own way.

But even if tomorrow's choices
    Now appear too vast,
The present is a gift—
    The joy you bring to it will last.

So while you weigh the future
    And its options you survey,
Don't be lost in choices—
    Make the most of your today.

BUT FOR CHANCE

But for chance, some paths don't cross,
    Some moments don't occur.
But for crystals formed in time,
    Some images just blur.

But for little accidents
    That turn our lives and change them,
Major forces wouldn't find
    Our dreams and rearrange them.

But for certain key events
    That interrupt our stride,
Worldly possibilities
    Would never seem so wide.

Losses, even setbacks,
    May propel our lives ahead.
Negatives may motivate
    And launch our goals instead.

Love may flourish, hopes may grow,
    And friendships may advance
Because of that imposing little
    Factor known as chance.

ENJOY TODAY

Enjoy today. Respect
    The gift of now.
Don't always wear tomorrow
    On your brow.

Enjoy the present.
    Sense and feel the light.
Observe the simple pleasures
    In your sight.

Enjoy the special seconds
    Slipping by,
The moments that your heart
    Can occupy.

Enjoy the loan of time
    That forms today.
Don't squander precious
    Memories away.

The future is comprised
    Of tiny treasures.
Today is all the future
    Ever measures.

HAPPINESS

When happiness comes
It comes in a song
With lyrics quite simple
And not very long.

If the tune seems elusive
Don't force it to flow;
When happiness comes
Your heart will know.

The melody's simple;
The words form with ease—
Life's magical moments
Provide all the keys.

Just cherish the beauty
Each moment is bringing—
You'll find that you're suddenly
Happily singing.

STAY CALM

Be calm; avoid
    The rumble of the day.
Let peace infuse
    Your atmosphere and stay.

Affirm a breath of air
    And let it free.
Allow your petty negatives
    To flee.

Assume another image
    In the whole,
A spark amidst the galaxies
    Your role.

Let your spirit wander
    From its cell,
That center where
    Identities must dwell,

And cast your glances
    Eagerly afar,
And lean a little thought
    Upon a star,

And pull a little pleasure
    From the day,
And rush a raft of worries
    All away.

TAKE TIME FOR YOURSELF

When it seems your life is racing,
    When your leisure slips away,
When the hurry and the worry
    Overshadow every day,

You must find some other meaning,
    Your essential worth renew.
You must lift your mood and spirit.
    You must take some time for you.

Place the needs of others second.
    Let the time that you divide
Turn into a day of wonder
    With a plan that you decide.

In the chaos and confusion,
    Step aside and find a place
You can peacefully escape
    To ease the stress, reduce the pace.

Act as if you're someone special.
    Do the things you have to do
To open up a little space
    And celebrate some time for you.

PRESENT PERFECT

If something rare was happening,
    I didn't notice when;
For nothing caught my senses
    In the commonplace of then.

The content of the moment
    Was conventional and normal.
The phrases and exchanges
    Filled an atmosphere informal.

But something special was in progress,
    Something rare and fleeting,
Something that in later thought
    Would often bear repeating.

Unexpected moments
    Can our memories endow.
Tomorrow finds its riches
    In the commonplace of now.

TAKE A MINUTE

Take a minute to reflect
   Upon the day just passed.
Take a minute to collect
   Sensations that will last.

Take a minute to enjoy
   The precious here and now.
Take a minute to explore
   The reasons why and how.

Take a minute to define
   The subtleties of love.
Take a minute to observe
   The mysteries above.

Take a minute to extract
   Some meaning from each other.
Take a special minute,
   Then another and another.

LISTEN TO YOUR LIFE

Listen to your life—
    Explore its details day by day.
Each moment is a special gift,
    Unique in its own way.

Don't fret about tomorrow
    Or surrender to the past.
Respect the day you're living in
    And make its magic last.

The present is a wondrous "now"—
    Each bird and bud amazes.
There is so much to focus on
    As years reveal their phases.

So guide the day from its beginning—
    Shape it to its end.
The gifts and opportunities
    And miracles will blend.

You'll find the moment you are in
    Is truly something rare.
Breathe in the air; expand your world;
    There isn't time to spare.

YOU'LL FIND THE ANSWER

There's a natural urgent desire
    To find all the answers you can.
The question of where you are going
    You ponder again and again.

Because certain answers elude you
    At various stages you reach,
You often miss one hidden message
    That life may be struggling to teach.

It is that the course of your future
    Resembles a ship in the sea.
The swells of the ocean around you
    May confuse you as you're drifting free.

But if each journey's prior condition
    Is seeing the most distant shore,
Then few journeys would ever be taken—
    Most dreams you would have to ignore.

So remember that distant horizons
    All exceed the fixed range of your sight.
And to make your important discoveries
    You must through life's turbulence fight.

For life is a series of tempests
    Obscuring the vision of some;
But if you can weather them patiently,
    Be assured that the answer will come.

DECISION

Decision is that
   Inner voice
That wrestles free
   Tomorrow's choice.

Decision is
   A sorting out
That looks for reasons,
   Handles doubt.

Decision finds
   A path to walk.
It weighs advice;
   It thrives on talk.

Decision deals
   Your future's hand
With strategies
   Both small and grand.

Decision gives
   Your goals their scope.
It channels wisdom,
   Measures hope.

Reflection scans
    Your dreams at play.
Decision takes you
    On your way.

BIG LITTLE CHOICES

How casual the choice
　　I made today.
It seemed completely
　　Insignificant.
How many forks in life
　　Do I assay
And quietly determine how my
　　Future will be spent.

In unassuming ways
　　Tomorrow's moments are decided.
Through minor course corrections,
　　Major changes are begun.
I seldom see the threads
　　By which I'm guided,
The paths which lead
　　To shadow or to sun.

How strange that such
　　Profound and weighty choices
Deceive us with their
　　Humble surface dress.
We never have
　　The courtesy of voices
Directing us, "This way
　　To happiness."

THERE'S A TIME FOR MOVING ON

You know it in your senses—
    You can feel it deep inside:
Your heart is getting restless—
    Your world is growing wide.

Your life is ripe for changing;
    Your dreams are full of hope.
You're ready to form new ambitions,
    Mount a higher slope.

You feel exhilaration—
    You sense your spirit rising.
You find the added energy
    As goals are galvanizing.

You're ready now for action,
    The fruit of all your planning.
You've thought it out and reasoned well,
    Tomorrow's promise scanning.

Nothing's ever guaranteed—
    Your doubts are never gone.
But in each life a time will come,
    A time for moving on.

I'M PROUD OF YOU

In many ways I'm proud of you—
    You've come a long, long way.
The growth in your abilities
    Has struck me day by day.

Each person has a goal to reach,
    A place they'd like to be,
A standard they aspire for,
    Results they'd like to see.

Some contests are for glory,
    Putting trophies on the shelf.
Others are the ones we wage
    For bettering the self.

It's not the stakes that count, but rather
    How we sense our movement;
And you are on a steady course
    Of rapid self-improvement.

The progress you are showing
    Makes me want to say aloud:
I'm happy where you're going,
    And you make me very proud.

PLAYING FIELD OF DREAMS

There is a field of life out there,
  A playing field of dreams.
You venture out upon this field,
  Explore its many themes.

You join a group, embrace a cause,
  Accept a certain role.
You order your priorities,
  Define a higher goal.

You are an individual,
  A fighting force of one.
You seize the possibilities;
  You learn to dodge and run.

You're there to learn about yourself,
  To survey your potential.
Initiative and independence
  Now become essential.

And as you play upon this field,
  It's key for you to know
We take a lot of pride in you,
  In watching how you grow.

We can't be certain from the sidelines
    What's the best for you.
We'll pull for you where possible
    And do what we can do.

You're not out there to live for us—
    Your life is yours to live.
We do not want to pressure you—
    Our love is all we give.

We honor and respect you for
    The goals that you proclaim.
Our hearts are always close to you
    As you pursue the game.

SEA OF CHOICES

In a sea of choices,
   I cast my nets
     Over the side,
Having planned my release,
   Timed my prior moves
     As best I can.
Soon I will pull in
   My yards of mesh,
Hoping upon hope
   That in the knotted tangle
     Of experience and decision
A measure of happiness
   Will come into my boat
And that in retrospect
   I will say that my catch
     Was a good one
And that time has been friendly
   To my choices.

PRAYER FOR TOMORROW

Lord, as I navigate
    On my life's journey,
Help me discover
    The right things to do.

Help me make choices
    That leave the world better.
Please, when I'm burdened,
    My spirits renew.

As I proceed on
    The course of my choosing,
Let me have goals
    I can firmly defend.

Let me become
    An example to others
With a real positive
    Message to send.

Help me survive
    On this difficult planet.
Let me have values
    As strong as the sun.

As I move forward,
    I'd like to look backward
And see how you've influenced
    All that I've done.

LIFE IS A WONDERFUL RIDE

I'm riding the crest of a wave,
  Standing firm, holding on
    For the run.
I'm splashed by the breezes,
  Awed by the rollers,
    Rinsed by the rays of the sun.

This may be the one
  Which will cruise all the way,
    Or one which will
      Dash me in foam;
But up in the challenge
  Of swells and salt vapors
    I savor the space
      That I roam.

I sometimes may crash
  In the perilous breakers,
    Dumped from a watery peak,
But soon I am back
  On the pulse of an ocean
    Carving a bubbly streak.

Though off in tomorrow,
    There may be a moment
        When I am consigned
            To the land,
Today I will keep on
    Pursuing the summit,
        Away from the warmth
            Of the sand.

And when I reflect
    On the life I have lived
        And the images past
            That I save,
I'll always remember
    The dreams that I carried
        High up
            On the crest of a wave.

ON THE EDGE OF ALL FUTURES

On the edge of all futures am I—
    On the fringe of a wind rushing by.
Like a leaf, I'm prepared to set sail,
    To encounter the breeze or the gale.

I'm perched on the border of change—
    My tomorrow I have to arrange.
Chance and hard work will soon blend,
    My future direction to send.

I'm not just a victim of fate,
    Though uncertainty has to await.
I'll work with the choices at hand
    And all that my life will demand.

I'll struggle to maintain control—
    I'll give it my heart and my soul.
When challenge looks me in the eye,
    I'll give it my very best try.

And as I set off on my flight,
    With dreams of fulfillment and light,
I'll hope that when clouds mar my way,
    I'll find an invincible day.

On the edge of all futures am I,
And my gift is this time rushing by.
Like a leaf, I have places to glide.
My God, what a wonderful ride!

TITLE INDEX

IDEA INDEX
(The real-life inspirations for selected poems)

Be A Source Of Light, p. 40: This poem is from my 2011 book, *Time Cries: A Poet's Response to 9/11/01*. It is my tribute to the first responders and unsung heroes of 9/11/01.

Be Yourself, p. 31: This poem was inspired by my wishes for my own children growing up, as well as the hopes of our German exchange student's mother in 1989 at the beginning of her teen son's four-month stay in the US.

Believe In Tomorrow, p. 88: Written for those times I feel I need a "do over" in life, a chance to relive a past moment and do something differently, but can't.

Big Little Choices, p. 112: Written about our son's college choice, toiled over for months and then disclosed to us at the last minute as the result of another's casual question to him, "Where are you going to college?" In unassuming ways we make some of the most life-changing decisions.

Don't Give Up, p. 57: Inspired by the story of a business associate's friend—a ballet dancer who prepared so hard for her job-of-a-lifetime with a major dance company that she developed leg injuries precluding her from pursuing this career opportunity.

Dream A New Day, p. 15: Inspired by a student whose parents had future plans for him in medicine that he did not share.

Follow Your Dreams, p. 4: Written for myself in 1976, when my career in creative writing was an urgent, but as yet undefined, dream.

Give It Your Best, p. 72: Originally entitled "You Gave It Your Best," this poem was inspired by the dedicated husband of a Parkinson's victim whose wife, a middle-aged professional, was near death. I retitled it years later when I learned that his wife, still living, had defied the odds and miraculously survived this serious crisis.

I Believe In You, p. 59: Written for my wife when she was responding to a major medical issue twenty-six years ago.

If You Have A Problem, p. 75: Written for someone who was suffering from serious psychological problems and was having difficulty confronting them.

Keep The Faith!, p. 85: Dedicated to victims of the 2008 financial collapse who lost their jobs, homes and savings, as well as those everywhere who are struggling to survive in a difficult world.

Life Is A Wonderful Ride, p. 120: I was watching the Australian surfing championships many years ago on TV when it occurred to me that this was a wonderful metaphor for life and an archetype for life's journey.

Life Isn't Always Easy, p. 66: Inspired by someone who needed three jobs to support a disabled husband and daughter, yet retained a gracious, uncomplaining disposition despite her challenging life.

Listen To Your Life, p. 107: Inspired by theologian Frederick Buechner's summary of life lessons learned and sermons preached in his memoir, *Now and Then*.

Present Perfect, p. 105: Inspired by tapping maple trees on Long Island with my two young children and the endless "wondrous things" my wife and I experienced as parents.

Take It One Step At A Time, p. 64: Written for a lovely and dedicated work associate during her courageous battle against vascular disease due to diabetes.

Take Time For Yourself, p. 104: Written for my wife, Sydney, who ably balanced a demanding career as small business owner with her roles as wonderfully caring mother, wife, daughter, and daughter-in-law—leaving very little time for herself.

That Strength From Within, p. 65: Dedicated to cancer victim Terry Fox and his Marathon Of Hope across Canada in 1980, as well as two other individuals who stood up courageously to extreme medical challenges at that time—an older friend who wouldn't surrender to disabling spinal osteoporosis and a young boy interviewed on TV with a rare aging disease, progeria, who had lived his full life by age twelve and showed uncommon valor in facing his terminal illness.

The Future Is Yours, p. 11: Originally titled "To My Son" but written with both my son and daughter in mind. Hence, the new title.

Things Will Get Better, p. 80: Written for a bright young person in the early 1980's who had to abort her almost completed college study due to federal budget cuts and loss of a scholarship.

Tomorrow's World Is You, p. 9: Written for my teen son and pre-teen daughter. The poem was originally entitled "Dear Teenager."

Try To Get Over It, p. 69: Inspired by a comedic Long Island mail clerk who was amazed at how excited some postal customers got over very minor issues. "Get over it" was his standard philosophical advice for disaffected patrons, muttered only after they left.

Turn It Around, p. 81: Inspired by the efforts of Columbine High School students to get beyond their 1999 tragedy and extract some positive meaning from their school's loss.

Yes I Can!, p. 71: This poem was the result of the cross-pollination of candidate Barack Obama's 2008 campaign slogan during the Texas primary, "Yes We Can," and a request at that same time by a Texas oncology nurse, Pat Bragg, for some inspirational poems to give to her support group for breast cancer survivors, LOL Sisterhood.

You're A Work In Progress, p. 25: Inspired by gifted singer Barbra Streisand's reply to an interviewer in the 1990's after he asked her if there was anything left for her to accomplish in her career, since she was at the pinnacle of success. She humbly said, "I am still a work in progress." Her wonderful answer applies to us all.

Bruce B. Wilmer was raised in Manhasset, New York and lives and works with his wife of 43 years, Sydney, in the Blue Ridge Mountains of western North Carolina. They started their poetry publishing business, Wilmer Graphics, in Huntington, New York in 1976 and raised their two children there. They relocated to North Carolina in 2003.

Bruce has chronicled people's emotions and feelings for over 36 years and touched millions around the world with his heartfelt and accessible poetry. He is the sole author of the company's Light Lines® Originals poetry products as well as the author of five other books of poetry. What he calls his "purposeful poetry" has been sold in thousands of stores of every type nationwide and in over 45 countries in two languages.

His Light Lines® Originals poems express thoughts of love, friendship, family, inspiration, encouragement and communication. The verses are typically displayed on various types of wall scrolls or carried on little laminated cards called Wallet Stuffers®. His books incorporate many of the poems found on his poetry products as well as others that go beyond their scope. Bruce's greatest satisfaction comes from hearing the heart-warming stories and personal responses of readers to his poems. Making a difference and inspiring others has always been important to him.

*My special thanks
to my wife, Sydney,
my parents, Florence and Will,
my eighth grade teacher, Dorothy Travis,
my high school English teacher, Katherine Elliott,
and my Archetypes professor, Norman O. Brown,
at the University of Rochester,
who all helped put poetry and creativity
into my life.*